IMAGES
of America

CHADRON

Student co-authors from Chadron State College: Dan Ascherl, Cale Bickerdyke, Michael Blount, Brice Bottorff, Sarah DeShaw, Darren Dobler, Megan Eklund, Mark Griffith, Dustin Harris, Adam Herring, Kent Kauffman, Trista Koncaba, Danielle Lee, Chris Merkel, Cassie Paul, Tina Pearson, Pierce Petersen, Lex Ravenscroft, Alva Roberts, Joel Schommer, Sully Serrano, Shane Teichmeier, Breanne Thompson, Stephanie Trask, Jared Webster, and Lisa Weedin (Chadron State College Composition Class, Spring 2004) pose inside the Dawes County Historical Museum. .

IMAGES
of America

CHADRON

Deb Carpenter and Ken Korte

ARCADIA
PUBLISHING

Published by Arcadia Publishing
Charleston, South Carolina

Library of Congress Catalog Card Number: 2004104151

For all general information contact Arcadia Publishing at:
Telephone 843-853-2070
Fax 843-853-0044
E-mail sales@arcadiapublishing.com
For customer service and orders:
Toll-Free 1-888-313-2665

Visit us on the Internet at www.arcadiapublishing.com

We would like to dedicate this book to the members of the Dawes County Historical Society. Thank you for donating your time, resources, and knowledge to our project. We certainly could not have done it without you!

CONTENTS

ACKNOWLEDGMENTS

The Chadron community was so very gracious to us throughout the entire process of compiling this pictorial history of Chadron. The Dawes County Historical Society opened the doors to the museum and allowed us to pick and choose photos from their vast collection. They volunteered their time and energy to help us gather information, and met with students on numerous occasions. We are grateful to Belle Lecher, Maggie Radcliffe, Lila Ahrens, Dean Carpenter, Rollin Curd, and Alice Faulk for their generosity and for their patience with us.

We are indebted to the following people who also provided photos, information, and background stories to give our project depth (listed in alphabetical order): Jan Adams, Dale and Pam Anderson, Chadron Chamber of Commerce, Hermie Cilek, Deb Cottier, Mr. Floyd Counts, Holly Counts, Lyle Goodman, Rodney Heesacker, Mabell Kadlecek, James Lees, Jeana Pickett, and Gail DeBuse Potter.

Thanks to Sarah Polak for continuing to make available the wonderful resources at the Mari Sandoz High Plains Heritage Center, and to Alex Smith for digitizing the photo collections. Alex deserves a bunch of gold stars for saying, "No problem," every time we brought in a new batch of photos or called to see if he could make a special trip in to scan something.

Another heartfelt thank you goes to Con Marshall for the photos, information, editing suggestions, and encouragement he so generously contributed.

Thanks to the Chadron State College Foundation for permission to use the Graves photo collection, the Slattery photo collection, and the miscellaneous boxes of college photos. We'd like to give a special thank you to everyone at Chadron State College who encouraged us to work on this book as a class project. We appreciate the assistance and guidance given by Terry Brennan, LuAnn Johnson, Glenda Gamby, and the rest of the staff of the Reta E. King Library. Thanks to Dr. Krepel, for reviewing the book proposal and contract.

To future students who benefit from our endeavors in the form of scholarships from book sales, we encourage you to foster the same appreciation we have for this special college community, the city of Chadron, and surrounding areas.

Finally, to the photographers, writers, and keepers of stories who passed on the legacy, thank you. We couldn't have completed this project without you.

–Deb Carpenter, Instructor, Chadron State College
–Ken Korte, Interim Director, Mari Sandoz High Plains Heritage Center
–Student co-authors, Chadron State College Composition Class, Spring 2004

INTRODUCTION

We can only conjecture what this area looked like before the late 1800s. Oral tradition, petroglyphs, and early written records reveal that nomadic tribes followed great buffalo herds and camped at various locations in this region. More recently, photographic records have given us a glimpse of the landscape and the lives of the people who made their mark on this region. That pictorial history is the one we wish to present here.

A photograph captures a small slice of the photographer's surroundings, from one vantage point, at a particular time and place. It often leaves out more than it depicts. This compilation will undoubtedly do the same, even though the work of several photographers gives the viewer many perspectives.

The Graves photos were taken by local professional photographers Ray and Faye Graves during the span of their careers. Ray died in 1916, but Faye continued the business until the 1940s, storing the photographic glass plates in the walls of her basement studio. These plates were later discovered and donated to Chadron State College by Don and Ruth Huls. Ray appreciated the historical era in which he lived, and he worked to capture some of that history on glass plates. He kept a variety of Native American regalia on hand, and often begged, cajoled, or bribed important figures to have their photographs taken. There is speculation that the picture of Red Cloud included in this book is the last photograph taken of the famous Indian Chief.

Judge Wallace Slattery was also fascinated with his era and the world around him. His work includes pictures of Native Americans, landscapes, buildings, and family.

The photos and postcards from the Dawes County Historical Society and photos from private family albums give the viewer an opportunity to look through many eyes, enabling one to envision the lives of farmers, ranchers, and merchants in the early days of Chadron. When the 100-year-old photographs, or past perceptions, are placed side by side with current photographs, the study is especially interesting.

That being said, Chadron is more than the pictures printed on these pages. It is also more than the buildings within the city limits. Chadron is comprised of people who came before us as well as those who now inhabit the land in and around the city itself.

What we now think of as "Chadron" was once unbroken prairie that was part of "White River Country," the general name for everything in northwestern Nebraska west of the big sandhills region. It was so named because White River was an important waterway to the fur trade.

Earliest fur trade efforts in what is now northwestern Nebraska began in 1841, when fur trade companies established trading posts on creeks near White River. The traders dealt mainly with the Oglala and Brule Sioux, trading goods primarily for tanned buffalo robes.

Conflicts over control of the land made this region a boiling plate, however. This affected trade and changed the makeup of the inhabitants of the land. Indian Agencies were formed, and military posts had to be established to police the agencies. Camp Robinson was established in 1873 to monitor Red Cloud's Oglala. Camp Sheridan followed close behind in 1874, when it was established to monitor Spotted Tail's Brule Indians.

One of the biggest single events which led to a change of inhabitants of this region, though, began in the summer of 1874, when George Armstrong Custer led an expedition into the Black Hills, which at the time belonged to the Sioux, and found gold. It's estimated that between November of 1875 and March of 1876, 10,000 people were drawn to the Black Hills. In 1875, President Ulysses S. Grant charged the military to keep settlers and miners out of Sioux territory, but the lure of gold was too great, and gold seekers disregarded the warnings.

On September 20, 1875, a Grand Council of about 20,000 Indians convened on White River in northwestern Nebraska, about eight miles from the Red Cloud Agency, to meet with government representatives, who offered to buy or rent the Black Hills. The Sioux refused. The military then withdrew their cavalry force from the Black Hills and settlers flooded in.

By 1876, the buffalo were gone, the 1868 treaty was abrogated, the Indians were moved to reservations, and the trading posts were closed for good.

The area was opened to homesteading, and in 1884, Fannie O'Linn settled on White River; the Sweat Colony settled on Bordeaux during that year, too, and both communities hoped that the coming railroad would bring prosperity. The Fremont, Elkhorn and Missouri Valley Railroad, however, had plans of its own, and bought ground where the city of Chadron is presently located. In August of 1885, the town of Chadron was officially founded.

The community changed as the inhabitants did. Hastily-built shacks were replaced by brick structures. Merchants built businesses; families built homes; the community built courthouses, jails, churches, schools, and a library. By 1910, after some competition with neighboring towns, the city of Chadron was selected as the site for the fourth Nebraska State Normal School.

Some things have changed considerably over the course of 100 and some odd years. The railroad brought prosperity to the community, but as time passed, the car became a standard mode of travel and the 18-wheeler took over the transportation of cattle and shipping of goods, so business dwindled for passenger trains, stock cars, and freight trains. Cattle barons had been able to make the best of the grassland available during the years when the buffalo herds were diminishing and before barbed wire crisscrossed the country. The railroad gave them access to the eastern markets, and the cattle business flourished. Now our farmers and ranchers are struggling.

Some things, however, have remained pretty much the same. Many people from neighboring towns, including Pine Ridge, still come to Chadron to do their shopping, conduct their business, and send their children to a school of higher learning.

All in all, Chadron is still a wonderful place to roam, camera in hand, to capture a slice of life.

One

EARLY CHADRON

Long before there was a Chadron State College or even a Wal-Mart, there were the Great Plains, buffalo, and Indians. The Crow Indians were one of the first tribes in the area. The Sioux then came to this area to hunt and forced out the Crow.

James Bordeaux and Louis Chartran, two of the first fur traders in this area, traded whiskey (also known as "milk"), guns, and American soldier uniforms for whatever goods the Indians could offer, mainly buffalo hides.

Once the area was opened up for homesteading, settlers moved in. Fannie O'Linn (who later became the first female attorney in Nebraska) chose a claim near the spot where White River joined Chadron Creek. She thought this location, where the railroad would most likely send a branch north to the Black Hills, would be the best place to develop a town.

She was right, but the price she set for the land was more than the railroad wanted to pay. They had someone come in and buy land a few miles away, much cheaper than Fannie's site. After they established this land as the location of the railhead, it was said that the town of O'Linn packed up and moved overnight approximately three miles down the road to the new location.

Fannie wanted to name the new town O'Linn, but it became known as Chadron, a derivative of fur trader Chartran's name. Chadron was founded on August 1, 1885. (Student co-authors: Trista Koncaba, Dan Ascherl, Chris Merkel, Pierce Petersen, and Alva Roberts.)

A press was often used to make compact bundles of furs and hides. This replica is at the Museum of the Fur Trade, located on the site of the Bordeaux Creek trading post. (Photo courtesy of Brice Bottorff.)

This postcard shows Little Bordeaux Creek, named after James Bordeaux, who was one of the prominent traders of the fur trade era. (Postcard courtesy of Dawes County Historical Society.)

A historical sign south of Chadron on Highway 385 marks the place where the employees of Lancaster P. Lupton built a trading post on "Chartran's Creek." (Photo courtesy of Deb Carpenter.)

This is an image of beautiful Chadron Creek. (Photo courtesy of CSC, Slattery Collection.)

Red Cloud, Chief of the Oglala Sioux, was born in 1822. He saw many changes in the land and people during his lifetime. Once free to hunt across the vast Plains, his people were eventually placed on reservations. Red Cloud's agency moved from near Fort Robinson to Pine Ridge, South Dakota. (Photo courtesy of CSC, Graves Collection.)

This postcard shows a Sioux medicine man in traditional dress. Note the buffalo horn headdress. (Postcard courtesy of Dawes County Historical Society.)

A SIOUX MEDICINE-MAN

This is another postcard depicting an unidentified Native American in traditional dress, this time holding a staff. Note the three young Native Americans off to the side, dressed in the style of their day. (Postcard courtesy of Dawes County Historical Society.)

This is an image of John Crow Likes Water, a showman. (Photo courtesy of CSC.)

Sioux warriors were part of the 1891 Fourth of July celebrations in Chadron. The Wounded Knee massacre occurred just six months prior to when this photo was taken. (Photo courtesy of CSC, Slattery Collection.)

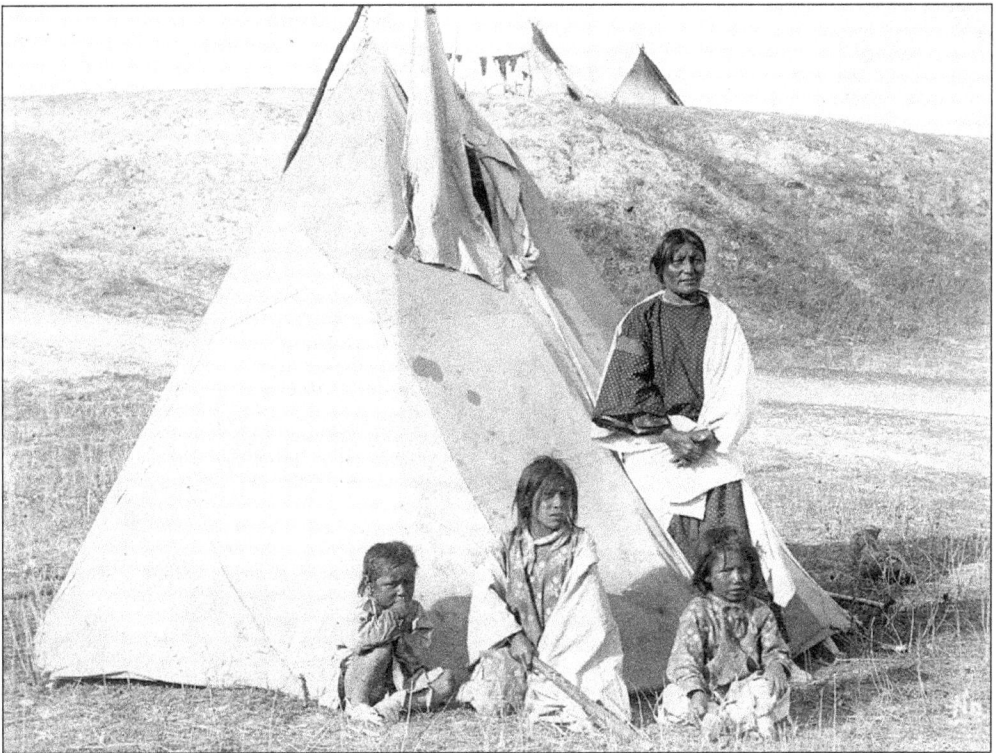

This image shows a Sioux camp east of Chadron. (Photo courtesy of CSC, Slattery Collection.)

Chief Dewey Beard was a survivor of both the Battle of Little Bighorn and the Wounded Knee Massacre. (Photo courtesy of CSC, Graves Collection.)

This image depicts Nelson's Outpost. In 1878, Peter B. Nelson settled on Bordeaux Creek, northwest of the current Museum of the Fur Trade. He built a store, post office, saloon, and stage station. He had a ranch and ran the Fort Robinson and Pine Ridge stage line. In 1888, Nelson built the Opera House in Chadron. (Photo courtesy of CSC, Graves Collection.)

This image captures the first court held in the new courthouse at Chadron. Fannie O'Linn, first female attorney in the state of Nebraska, is seated at a table in the courthouse. Notice her reflection in the highly polished table. (Photo courtesy of Dawes County Historical Society.)

This is the gravesite of Daniel Egbert O'Linn, who accidentally shot himself. "Bert" was the oldest son of Fannie O'Linn. The grave, near O'Linn, was eventually moved to the family burial plot at Blair, Nebraska. (Photo courtesy of Con Marshall.)

Chadron State College students Dan Ascherl and Chris Merkel stand with the actual O'Linn Post Office sign, which is housed at the Dawes County Historical Museum. Above the sign are copies of books on Nebraska post offices, which W.A. Woodward of Chadron compiled by county. (Photo courtesy of Trista Koncaba.)

18

Chadron State College student Chris Merkel points to where the town of O'Linn once stood. (Photo courtesy of Trista Koncaba.)

Dawes County resident Lyle Goodman stands to the front and side of Dakota Junction. (Photo courtesy of Trista Koncaba.)

This is a view of Chadron Congregational Academy in the 1890s. (Photo courtesy of CSC, Slattery Collection.)

This postcard declares "Some Town, 20 Years Ago." (Postcard courtesy of Dawes County Historical Society.)

The old Gold Bar Saloon was located on the corner of Second and Main. Inside, it boasted a bar, gambling room, dance hall, and vaudeville stage. Outside, they kept a cage of wildcats on the walkway. (Photo courtesy of Dawes County Historical Society.)

Man and horse pose outside the historic Rex Theater. The Rex was built in 1918 at 246 Main Street. It showed motion pictures rather than presenting live entertainment. The horse's name was Star April Fool because he was born April 1, 1912. His owner was George C. Snow. (Photo courtesy of CSC, Graves Collection.)

This image depicts early Chadron transportation. The team and wagon are on the street in front of Chadron's Book and Job Office. (Photo courtesy of CSC, Graves Collection.)

People of the Chadron community enjoyed their neighbors and made time for picnics. (Photo courtesy of CSC, Graves Collection.)

This is an example of an early version of an 18-wheeler. (Photo courtesy of CSC, Graves Collection.)

Taken at Chadron June 24, 1905, this photo shows the following, from left to right: (back row) Walks Fast, Afraid, Dr. Davis, and George Fire Thunder; (middle row) Billy "the Bear" Iaeger and Red Cloud; (front row) Freddy Davis and Fred Wilke. (Photo courtesy of Dawes County Historical Society.)

23

FORT ROBINSON & PINE RIDGE STAGE LINE.

From F. Robinson   *to Pine Ridge*

Aug 22 188

PASSENGERS' NAMES.	No. of Seats.	Extra Bag'ge.	WHERE FROM.	WHERE TO.	Aml. Paid.	Collect.	BY WHOM RECEIVED.

EXPRESS.

ARTICLE.	Weight.	From Whom or Where.	ADDRESS.	DESTINATION.	Advance.	Our Charges.	Collect.	Prepaid.
Trunk		Red Cloud		Pine Ridge		Up Passenger		

This is a ledger sheet from the Fort Robinson to Pine Ridge Stage Line, August 22, 1881. Notice Red Cloud's name. (Courtesy of Dawes County Historical Society.)

Two

CATTLEMEN AND SETTLERS

During the period from 1850 to 1880, life in the Great Plains underwent a rapid transition. As the vast free-roaming buffalo herds gave way to Texas longhorns arriving by the thousands, Native Americans were increasingly displaced by whites. Culture in the region became that of the cattleman.

Western Nebraska and most certainly Dawes County became an ideal destination for southern cattle herds. Cattle in the Nebraska Territory numbered 37,197 in the year 1860, and by 1880 had increased to 1,113,247. These herds were propelled by the grassy expanses of virtually unclaimed land where cattle could roam freely.

Nearby Indian agencies provided a steady demand for beef to fill their issues. Area cattlemen supplied approximately 9,000,000 pounds per year or around 13,000 head to these agencies. Local military posts provided additional demand.

By 1885 the Fremont, Elkhorn and Missouri Valley Railroad had reached Chadron. On August 15, 1885 the first train of cattle was shipped to the Chicago market by Charles Coffee, a prominent area cattleman.

However, the free-range utopia wouldn't last forever. The arrival of the railroad in the mid-1880s saw farmers and settlers pouring into the area, armed with valid titles to land previously considered public domain. Tensions between cattlemen and "squatters," or grangers, ensued. It was not long before cattlemen recognized the changing times and submitted to permanent settlement or moved on. (Student co-authors: Stephanie Trask, Cale Bickerdyke, Adam Herring, Darren Dobler, and Joel Schommer.)

Crawford in 1890 was one of the wildest cattle towns in the area, salted with military men from nearby Fort Robinson, as well as traders, cowboys, and run-off from the Red Cloud Indian Agency. (Photo courtesy of Dawes County Historical Society.)

Every spring and fall, the local cattlemen and their hired hands spent weeks gathering, sorting, and branding their cattle scattered by the thousands across miles of open range. No doubt, the chuck wagon was a welcome sight during a long grueling work day. (Postcard courtesy of Dawes County Historical Society.)

Far from home, round-up hands detained their mounts in makeshift rope corrals for the night. (Postcard courtesy of Dawes County Historical Society.)

In this image, a crude fence contains cattle on the Evans ranch near Belmont in 1902. (Photo courtesy of Dawes County Historical Society.)

Two wealthy entrepreneurs from Omaha, A.W. Reikman and Mr. May, arrived in the area in the mid-1880s. They purchased several homesteads to form the 10,000-acre UR Ranch. Pictured here are John Schildhauer (center, on horse), who was the 17-year foreman of the UR, and his wife and eight children. The mounted man to the right is John Cilek, who would become the subsequent foreman. This photo was taken in 1903. (Photo courtesy of Hermie Cilek.)

In this image, men of Chaulk and Birdsall Contractors operate an elevating grader, possibly during the construction of the Chadron dam in 1912. A.W. Reikman of the UR stands to the right. (Photo courtesy of Dawes County Historical Society.)

This picture was taken on Al Sperling's portion of the original UR after it was dissolved into neighboring ranches. Here, it is still populated with shorthorns, the breed stocked by Reikman and May. (Photo courtesy of Dawes County Historical Society.)

After a successful sharp-shooting venture, three men take a break to replenish supplies at the ranch smokehouse. (Photo courtesy of CSC, Slattery Collection.)

Early settlers, the Bare family, marvel at the ocean of grain—in which it was not unusual to lose small children. (Photo courtesy of Dale Anderson.)

30

Levi G. Sweat was leader of the "Sweat Colony," a group of 20 individuals and their families from Gentry County, Missouri, who arrived in Valentine by train in 1884. They took out claims in the new territory, sight unseen, and traveled through Pine Ridge to the Bordeaux and Chadron valleys by wagon train. Ed Egan arrived in the area in their company and became founder of the first Chadron newspaper. He wrote ". . . The sturdy integrity of the men of the Sweat Colony was a potent factor in shaping the affairs of the fast-settling country . . . and the pictures in the campfire dreams came true in the years of the Dawes County history." (Photo courtesy of Dawes County Historical Society.)

Mrs. Anderson feeds the chickens while husband, John, looks on from the doorway of the barn. Poultry and eggs, along with other farm produce, were important to early homesteaders—both as food and as a source of income from local markets. (Photo courtesy of Dale Anderson.)

A couple head southwest in their buggy toward Bordeaux Creek. (Photo courtesy of Dale Anderson.)

A homesteader uses a breaking plow on virgin prairie. (Photo courtesy of Dale Anderson.)

This picture of the A.H. Smith barn and horses was taken around 1903. (Photo courtesy of Dawes County Historical Society.)

This photo captures four generations of the Lecher family at their homestead, around 1909. The second story and the room to the left were added to the original house as the family grew. For years, Casper Lecher, the man leaning against the porch support on the left, supplied ice cut from a nearby creek to the people of Chadron. (Photo courtesy of Belle Lecher.)

Dressed in their Sunday finery, the Hans Rissell family from Sweden proudly displays their livestock, corrals, buildings, and one gun on their homestead in southern Dawes County. It was a common practice among homesteaders at the time to include all of their most valued possessions in the family photo. These pictures were then sent to relatives back east to show how the family was prospering. (Photo courtesy of Dawes County Museum.)

This photo depicts the practice of sawing lumber down at Bordeaux Station. (Photo courtesy of Dale Anderson.)

Threshing grain by horse power was another necessary activity at the time. (Photo courtesy of Dale Anderson.)

Another method of threshing was through the use of steam power. Due to a shortage of machines, it was sometimes winter before grain was threshed. (Photo courtesy of Dale Anderson.)

Members of the Harvey Anderson family pose in front of their home. An onlooker gets a view from the windmill, a vital water source on most homesteads. (Photo courtesy of Dale Anderson.)

This photo shows horses being used to drill a well on Charlie Siefer's place in 1902. (Photo courtesy of Dawes County Historical Society.)

A settler at the Harvey Anderson homestead dips seed potatoes, possibly in formaldehyde, to prevent "scab." (Photo courtesy of Dale Anderson.)

This bridge, made of wagon boxes, was used to move hogs to market. (Photo courtesy of Dale Anderson.)

This springboard wagon was used as a method of transportation on early Chadron trails. (Postcard courtesy of Dawes County Historical Society.)

A church on the ranch near Adaton is seen here. Due to the distances between settlements and limited transportation, schools and churches were built on individual ranches and served the occupying families and some of the surrounding neighbors. (Postcard courtesy of Dawes County Historical Society.)

This country was known for its Hereford cattle. The herd seen here was photographed near Adaton. (Photo courtesy of CSC, Graves Collection.)

The Chadron Hereford show flourished during the late 1940s and early 1950s. This photograph shows a popularly-displayed car ornament from that era, when it was reported that there were more registered Hereford producers within 100 miles of Chadron than anywhere else. (Photo courtesy of Con Marshall.)

This is a 1948 picture of the original Ormesher slaughterhouse located just north of Chadron, which supplied the beef for Ormesher's Meat Market in town. (Photo courtesy of Dawes County Historical Society.)

Smiling meat cutters and clerks at the Ormesher Meat Market, from left to right, are as follows: W.A. Potts, Tom Ormesher, Roy Hezies, Dan Burns, Ralph Ormesher, and Ted Ormesher. The photo was taken around 1920. (Photo courtesy of Dawes County Historical Society.)

41

Pictured here are members of the Dahlman Cowboy Quartet. James C. Dahlman (center) arrived in Nebraska from Texas around 1874, after allegedly killing his brother-in-law. Described by a friend as the "hardest riding, squarest, and best cowman," the young Dahlman soon became foreman of the famous Newman ranch. He moved to Chadron and became the first sheriff of Dawes County. He also served as mayor of Chadron (1894–1896) and eventually mayor of Omaha. (Photo courtesy of Dawes County Historical Society.)

Lou Nixon (*right*) and Ray Graves, the studio photographer of Chadron's early years, used to amuse themselves by dressing up and taking pictures of one another. Here Nixon poses in the regalia of an Indian chief. (Photo courtesy of CSC, Graves Collection.)

Lou Nixon, dressed as a cowpuncher, was in fact a life-long rancher. He was born in 1891 in a homestead dug-out, the youngest of eight children. His father hauled freight in a horse-drawn wagon from the rail's end at Valentine to the town of Wayside, northwest of Chadron. (Photo courtesy of CSC, Graves Collection.)

In this picture, taken at the Dawes County Fair Rodeo in 1948, the world champion bronc rider Turk Greenough of Red Lodge, Montana, prepares for a wild ride with the aid of a number of fellow cowboys. (Photo courtesy of Dawes County Historical Society.)

Famous rodeo clown and bull rider "Benny Bender" was seriously injured while bull riding at the 1948 rodeo. (Photo courtesy of Dawes County Historical Society.)

Three

RAILS AND TRAILS

Chadron's history was a result of not only the township, but its "rails and trails." Several contributors were a 1,000-mile race of steeds, the gouging trudge of many feet across the years, and a locomotive bed of steel.

Word of the legendary Chadron to Chicago Horse Race began its rapid circulation through newspapers as a practical joke started by John G. Maher, a Chadron resident.

Maher liked to print exaggerated stories of pioneer life to amaze eastern readers. Now Chadron was faced with a decision: print a rebuttal to the false story and infuriate readers worldwide, or make the seemingly impossible feat a reality. Chadron citizens led by L.J.F. Iaeger met and decided that their only option was to produce the 1,000-mile horse race.

The trails of the area were equally important. In 1874, nearly 1,000 troops followed the Fort Laramie-Fort Robinson Trail to establish the camps at Sheridan and Robinson to oversee the Red Cloud and Spotted Tail Agencies. Because of the gold discovery in Deadwood, the Sidney-Deadwood Trail was a well-populated "highway." Freight wagons, stagecoaches, and horseback riders were the main traffic on the trail.

Chadron's history is also deeply imbedded in the area's railroad. From its beginnings as the Fremont, Elkhorn and Missouri Valley Railroad, to the Chicago and North Western, to the Burlington Northern and Santa Fe, the railroad has played a key role in Chadron's development as a "railroad town." (Student co-authors: Danielle Lee, Cassie Paul, Megan Eklund, Jared Webster, and Michael Blount.)

There is still evidence of the old Indian travois trails. Indians used to pull loads behind their dogs or horses. The travois consisted of two trailing poles with a platform or net to carry the load, and left two distinct marks on the path. (Photo courtesy of Mabell Kadlecek.)

"The Crossing of Trails" is allegedly where the Sidney-Deadwood and Fort Laramie-Fort Robinson trails crossed. (Photo courtesy of Danielle Lee.)

This is an example of early area transportation you might find traveling the Sidney-Deadwood Trail. (Photo courtesy of Dale Anderson.)

This historical marker is used to signify the 265-mile Sidney-Deadwood Trail (referred to here as the Sidney-Black Hills Trail) On August 20, 1885, the Sidney-Deadwood stage changed railroad connections from Sidney to Chadron. It is said that 22 million pounds of freight and $200,000 worth of gold were shipped across the trail over the course of its existence. (Photo courtesy of Danielle Lee.)

The Fort Laramie-Fort Robinson Trail linked Fort Laramie to outposts in the Pine Ridge area. On December 29, 1890, General Nelson A. Miles passed through Chadron on this trail to take command of troops in the field. (Photo courtesy of Danielle Lee.)

As a joke to eastern readers, John G. Maher started the false "Chadron to Chicago Horse Race" story circulating through newspapers. The story swept through the United States and parts of Europe. (Photo courtesy of Dawes County Historical Society.)

The Blaine Hotel was the starting point of the 1,000-mile Chadron to Chicago Horse Race of 1893. (Postcard courtesy of Dawes County Historical Society.)

"Billy the Bear" Iaeger (left) and James C. Dahlman (right) in Omaha, headed up the Chadron to Chicago Horse Race committee. The committee was formed to solve the problem that John Maher had caused by circulating the false story. (Photo courtesy of Dawes County Historical Society.)

The *Dawes County Journal* (Friday, June 16, 1893, page 1) quoted J.O. Hartzell at the start of the Chadron to Chicago Horse Race as saying, "Boys: the hour has now arrived for the cowboy race from Chadron to Chicago to start. I trust you will take good care of your horses, and I know you will conduct yourselves as gentlemen and uphold the good name of Chadron and the state of Nebraska." (Photo courtesy of Dawes County Historical Society.)

Doc Middleton is shown outside Buffalo Bill Cody's tent at the finish of the Chadron to Chicago Horse Race on the horse "Bay Minnie." Middleton, a notorious horse thief, was one of the last participants to finish the race. (Photo courtesy of Dawes County Historical Society.)

Joe Gillespie and Charles Smith rest at the finish line of the Chadron to Chicago Horse Race. Gillespie and Smith won first and second place, respectively, due to the disqualification of the original first place rider, John Berry. (Photo courtesy of Dawes County Historical Society.)

Joe Gillespie won this Colt revolver upon completing the 1,000-mile horse race. The revolver was donated by Buffalo Bill Cody. (Photo courtesy of Dawes County Historical Society.)

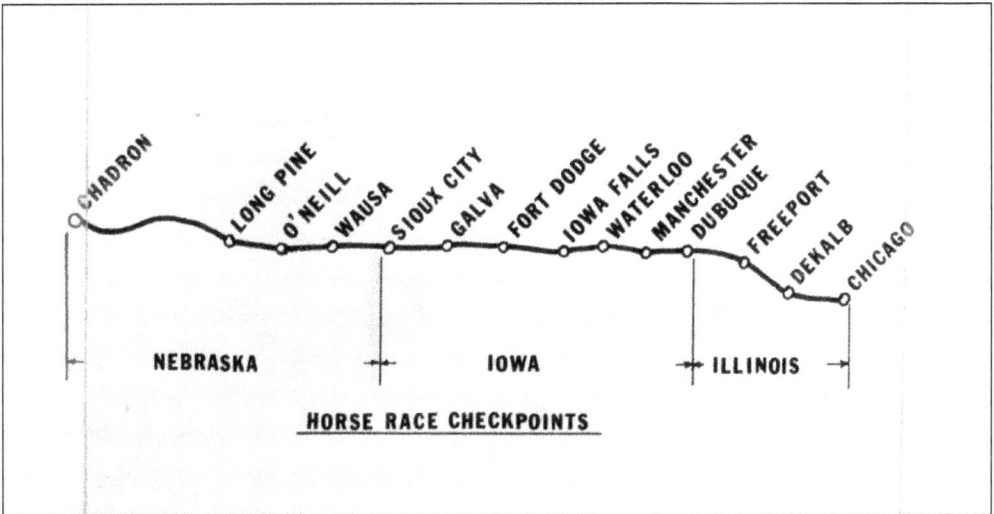

The 1,000-mile horse race was mapped out starting in Chadron and going through various towns, such as Sioux City and Fort Dodge, Iowa. (Photo courtesy of Dawes County Historical Society.)

Since the 1893 horse race, there have been two re-enactments. Don Berlie, riding King Pine; Milton Grantham, riding Apache; Raymond Eaton, riding Bunny; and Bill Kohler, riding Tony were the four riders who participated in Chadron's Silver Jubilee Celebration in 1960. (Photo courtesy of Dawes County Historical Society.)

Bob Bishop (publisher of *Nebraska Farmer*) and Orla Rucker were the drivers for the Silver Jubilee Celebration. Bishop and Rucker drove the four riders and their horses to the checkpoints, then let them out to ride into the towns for celebrations. (Photo courtesy of Dawes County Historical Society.)

54

John Anderson is pictured with his wife and their son, Harvey, at Bordeaux Station on the Fremont, Elkhorn and Missouri Valley Railroad. Note the track immediately in front of the station. This photo was taken in 1888. (Photo courtesy of Dale Anderson.)

The Bordeaux Station/Depot, several miles east of Chadron, was used by the Fremont, Elkhorn and Missouri Valley Railroad. This photo was taken in the 1890s. (Photo courtesy of Dale Anderson.)

Valentine, Nebraska, was the end of the line until 1885, when the line was completed to the rail terminal of Chadron. (Photo courtesy of Dawes County Historical Society.)

Railroad workers make their way through the Chadron railroad yards. The freight office is seen on the left. (Postcard courtesy of Dawes County Historical Society.)

The Roundhouse, completed on October 29, 1885, made Chadron more than just another stop on the line. It made Chadron a terminus. These men are standing in the machine shop. (Photo courtesy of Dawes County Historical Society.)

The Chicago and North Western Railroad Depot was established in 1903. (Postcard courtesy of Dawes County Historical Society.)

Engine 1255, along with many other trains, made its way through Chadron in the early years of the railroad. This picture was taken in 1911. (Photo courtesy of Dawes County Historical Society.)

Engine 1185 and its crew are stopped at the Chadron train depot in this 1911 photograph. In 1958, the Chicago and North Western Railroad sold its tracks to the Black Hills Central Railroad. (Photo courtesy of Dawes County Historical Society.)

The crew of Engine 1813 pose for a picture in July of 1962. (Photo courtesy of Dawes County Historical Society.)

William Spencer and Roy Moore talk business in Chadron's railroad office. (Photo courtesy of Dawes County Historical Society.)

The Chadron Roundhouse workers stand in front of the original facility. "Veteran 4-4-0s" are seen in the stalls behind them. This facility was updated in 1903 with the installation of a new 70-foot turntable, coal chutes, and drop pit. (Photo courtesy of Dawes County Historical Society.)

Oops! Workers stand by after Engine 530 ran off the tracks inside of the Chadron turntable. (Postcard courtesy of Dawes County Historical Society.)

Spectators gather in the aftermath of the devastating roundhouse fire, sometime between 1896 and 1898. From left to right, the men in the photo are as follows: Carter, machinist; Bunten, carpenter; Jancik, helper; Jim Ball, boiler washer; John R. Campbell; three unknown men; Chet Swampson, apprentice; unknown; Mel Wadley, blacksmith; Lzicor, apprentice; Fred Sharrer, supply man; unknown; George Strickland, machinist; and Bill Campbell in the foreground. (Photo courtesy of Dale Anderson.)

On August 6, 1910, the roundhouse and surrounding shops, all valued at half a million dollars, were destroyed by fire. (Photo courtesy of Dawes County Historical Society.)

Campaign of 1896

X Korns -Editor of Chadrc

X W.J.Bryan

Democratic Presidential candidate, William Jennings Bryan, and campaign group of 1896 pose on the FE&MV for a campaign picture. (Photo courtesy of Dawes County Historical Society.)

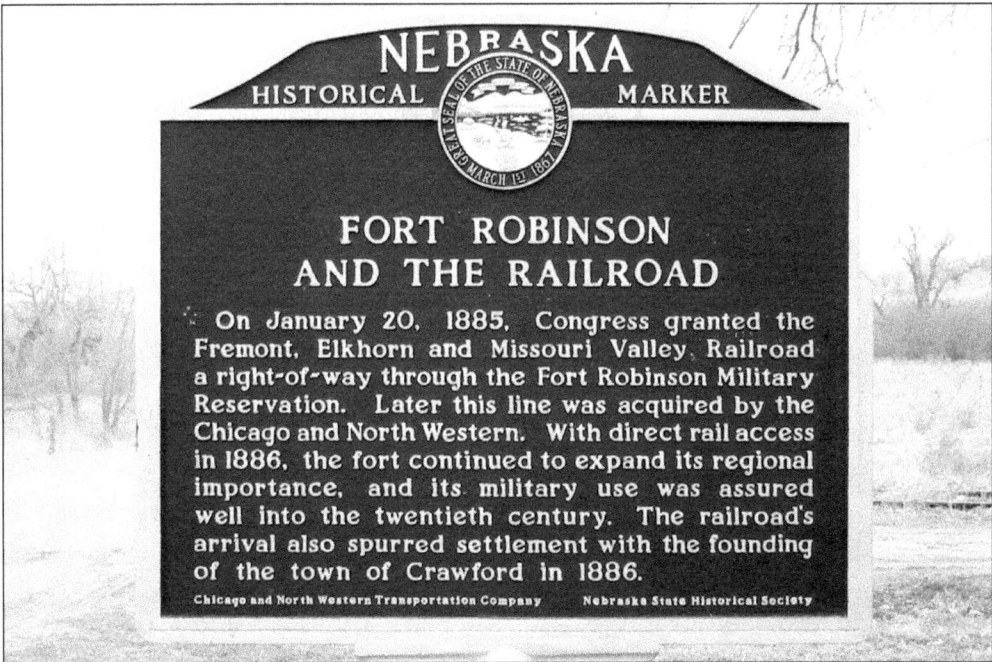

The Nebraska State Historical Society erected this marker to acknowledge the importance of the railroad to Fort Robinson. (Photo courtesy of Danielle Lee.)

Rail lines were the vital arteries through the area. Fort Robinson used the rails for transportation not only to the Fort, but also through it. (Photo courtesy of Danielle Lee.)

The Belmont Tunnel was built by the Burlington Railroad in 1888–1890. It is a 750-foot tunnel located about 15 miles south of Crawford, Nebraska. (Postcard courtesy of Dawes County Historical Society.)

Though it is not in use today, the Belmont Tunnel still stands as Nebraska's only tunnel. (Photo courtesy of Danielle Lee.)

Engine 2320 pushes its way past tall snow drifts caused by the 1949 blizzard. (Photo courtesy of Dawes County Historical Society.)

The snow took its toll on the rails. In this image, men help clear the tracks so that a train can plow its way through the 1949 blizzard. (Photo courtesy of Dawes County Historical Society.)

A rotary snow plow makes its way through the enormous drifts caused by the 1949 blizzard. (Photo courtesy of Dawes County Historical Society.)

It is hard to imagine how high these drifts were until you see someone standing on the tracks. (Photo courtesy of Dawes County Historical Society.)

On June 15, 1921, Casper to Chadron No. 606 went over Cottonwood Creek and fell through the bridge. People speculated that high water a week earlier had caused bridge supports to weaken. Five people were killed and 14 injured in this tragic wreck near Whitney, Nebraska. (Postcards courtesy of Dawes County Historical Society.)

Marcus Cain, known as "the man who loved trains," stands on top of a box car. (Photo courtesy of Dawes County Historical Society.)

LEAVING, TOWN.

The last passenger train to leave Chadron, July 6, 1958, was the Chicago and North Western's No. 14. (Photo courtesy of Dawes County Historical Society.)

Four

CHANGING FACES

As time has advanced, so have the towns of the west, and Chadron is no exception. Starting as a mere end to the railroad, with more saloons than houses, Chadron has grown into a center of higher learning for the west. This change has not been easy. In 1949, a blizzard struck the town, leaving it buried under five feet of snow and stranding the town's residents for several days. Faced with the hardships of the west's wild weather and other influencing factors, Chadron has managed to hold together and become the town it is today.

Chadron is known for its first residents, as well. It was the hometown of former Omaha Mayor James Dahlman, who served as sheriff and mayor when he lived in Chadron. Fannie O'Linn was the first female attorney in Nebraska; Mr. Jim Mears was Chadron's first mayor.

Time passes and the faces of the people and the land change. A major change in the landscape was the addition of Chadron State College, once known as Chadron State Normal College. Chadron State College has seen an increase in enrollment from 100 to over 3,000 students, all helping to drive Chadron into the future. Chadron certainly is a place of change and will continue to change as the years go by. (Student co-authors: Breanne Thompson, Sully Serrano, Lisa Weedin, Dustin Harris, and Shane Teichmeier.)

Established in 1885, Chadron quickly grew as a town. By 1887, it covered several acres. (Photo courtesy of Dawes County Historical Society.)

This photo shows Henry Ormesher and his meat market in early 1900 on Main Street. Henry's meat market was kept busy with the high volume of cattle that was moved through Chadron by rail. In those days, steak was sold for 10¢ a pound at the Ormesher butcher shop. (Photo courtesy of Dawes County Historical Society.)

On the far left is P.W. Hennessy, owner of the Hennessy Book and News Company. (Photo courtesy of Dawes County Historical Society.)

Pictured is the south side of 2nd Street in the early 1900s. The building on the far left side housed one of the three newspapers in print in Chadron at this time. (Photo courtesy of Dawes County Historical Society.)

The streets of Chadron remained dirt roads until April of 1920, when the city voted to pave them. (Photo courtesy of Dawes County Historical Society.)

A car stuck in the mud was a common site to see after heavy rainfall in Chadron. This photo was taken in the Kenwood area. (Photo courtesy of Dawes County Historical Society.)

This postcard looks south on Main Street toward "C" Hill. Dating from the early 1920s, it depicts a corner drug store and a barrel in the middle of the street advertising baseball. (Postcard courtesy of Dawes County Historical Society.)

The vantage point here is from 2nd Street, looking east from Morehead. The Reitz and Crites Lumber and Coal building is pictured on the left side of the street. (Photo courtesy of Dawes County Historical Society.)

This 1912 bird's-eye view of Chadron looks south from the courthouse toward the college. (Photo courtesy of Dawes County Historical Society.)

This is a photo of the city of Chadron, looking north from the college toward downtown. (Photo courtesy of Dawes County Historical Society.)

Another bird's-eye view of Chadron is seen here. Pictured in the foreground is the Congregational Academy, which was destroyed by fire in 1892. (Photo courtesy of Dawes County Historical Society.)

In this bird's-eye view of early Chadron, the original courthouse is visible on the far left. (Photo courtesy of Dawes County Historical Society.)

A team of horses pulls a wagon carrying gasoline across 2nd Street, in front of the Blaine Hotel. This photo was taken in 1888. (Photo courtesy of Rodney Heesacker.)

Three little girls cross what is now Chadron Avenue at 2nd Street. (Photo courtesy of Rodney Heesacker.)

Compare the crossroads of Chadron Avenue and 2nd Street as it appeared in 1888 (*top photo*) with how it appears in 2004. (Photo courtesy of Breanne Thompson.)

The United States Federal Building was built in 1919 and housed the Chadron Post Office as well as the federal offices. An addition was built in 1997 to help with the increasing amount of mail. The "bell tower" on the building is actually a restroom. (Photo courtesy of Dawes County Historical Society.)

This is Chadron's post office today. (Photo courtesy of Breanne Thompson.)

PUBLIC LIBRARY.
CHADRON, NEB.

As the town of Chadron progressed toward becoming a center of civilization in western Nebraska, the need for a library was realized. After Mayor Finnegan wrote to Andrew Carnegie for financial assistance to build a public library, Mr. Carnegie granted the request on March 4, 1910, with two conditions. First, the library must raise $500 annually. Second, the library board must find a suitable site. After an extensive debate over a potential site, the library opened its doors on February 13, 1912, at 507 Bordeaux. Mrs. Elizabeth O'Linn Smith was the librarian. (Postcard courtesy of Dawes County Historical Society.)

The Chadron Public Library continues serving the needs of the community. (Photo Courtesy of Breanne Thompson.).

Chadron's first church, the Congregational Church of Chadron, was built in the fall of 1885 and stood until 1959 when the new building (shown here) was completed. This church's first minister, Reverend G.J. Powell, began his ministry in 1887. It was Reverend Powell who led the effort to establish the Congregational Academy that later became a normal school and today is Chadron State College. (Photo courtesy of Breanne Thompson.)

The Congregational church was first located at 3rd Street and Chadron Avenue, with the courthouse to the south. The church was later moved to Kenwood and the new church (*top photo*) was built. (Postcard courtesy of Dawes County Historical Society.)

Grace Episcopal Church was organized in February of 1887. The original part of the building was completed on January 6, 1889. The addition was built on at a later time, but the stonework matched perfectly with the original building. (Postcard courtesy of Dawes County Historical Society.)

Beginning on March 2, 1886, Catholic services were held at Mrs. Margaret Murphy's home, before the King Street site was chosen for the first Catholic church in Chadron. This building was destroyed by fire December 15, 1927. (Postcard courtesy of Dawes County Historical Society.)

Chadron's Frank Alzicar is pictured in his store around 1900. Frank's store was originally Joe Lichty's Barber Shop. (Photo courtesy of Dawes County Historical Society.).

This is the Chadron Mill in the early 1920s. Opened in 1889, the Chadron Flour Mill was known throughout the tri-state area for its brand of flour named "Lily White." The mill burned down in 1962. (Photo courtesy of Dawes County Historical Society.)

This is the Henry Maika Drug Store on Main Street. (Photo courtesy of Dawes County Historical Society.)

This photo shows an early mercantile store in downtown Chadron. (Photo courtesy of Dawes County Historical Society.)

Boy and dog, both unidentified, are pictured outside a Chadron café. (Photo courtesy of Rodney Heesacker.)

This June 15, 1924, photo pictures Evelyn, Leslie, and Melvin with their stepmother Bessie Serbousek Reeves. (Photo courtesy of Dawes County Museum.)

This is the Slattery family of Chadron. Maria Slattery is on the far left. Maude and Ernest Slattery are on the right. (Photo courtesy of CSC, Slattery Collection.)

The Erlewine house, located at 2nd and Shelton, is pictured in the 1930s. (Photo courtesy of Dawes County Historical Society.)

On April 8, 1904, the O'Hanlon hotel building just off Main Street was purchased and remodeled by the railroad. It was turned into a YMCA and opened to the public. (Postcard courtesy of Dawes County Historical Society.)

The old YMCA is now the Olde Main Street Inn (at 115 Main Street). This is how it looks in 2004. (Photo courtesy of Breanne Thompson.)

This photo shows the Western Public Service County Building in early Chadron. (Photo courtesy of Dawes County Historical Society.)

This is a picture of Freed's furniture store as seen in the 1950s. The corner was remodeled and the second story addition was put on above the center section in April of 1960. Freed's furniture store was located on 2nd Street. (Photo courtesy of Dawes County Historical Society.)

This photo, taken in May of 1907, shows the office of the *Chadron Journal*. In 1886, the Chadron Post Office operated out of the bottom floor while the *Journal* was printed on the top floor. (Photo courtesy of Dawes County Historical Society.)

The *Chadron Record* Building, built in 1888, is one of Chadron's oldest buildings. The original horse trough still remains on the west side of the building, and the second floor remains in its original condition. The *Chadron Record* was one of the original five newspapers in the early Chadron community, and is the only city newspaper today. (Photo courtesy of Breanne Thompson.)

The Chadron City Volunteer Fire Department was formed in 1886 and has served continually since. (Photo courtesy of Dawes County Historical Society.)

This is the Farmer's Union Store in early Chadron. Pictured on the far left is Bernice Carpenter, a clerk. (Photo courtesy of Dawes County Historical Society.)

Construction on this building, referred to as the "New Courthouse," began in 1935 and was completed in 1936. It was occupied for the first time on December 4, 1936, and is characterized by its symmetrical and sold mass. The buttress-like pilasters accent its architectural character. (Photo courtesy of Breanne Thompson.)

The Dawes County Courthouse was built in 1889 in Chadron. It was located between present-day 3rd and 4th Streets on Main Street. The courthouse was a symbol of law and order in a wild west community. It was later torn down because there was not enough jail space. Rather than building a separate jail, the decision was made to build an entirely new courthouse with additional jail space. (Photo courtesy of Dawes County Historical Society.)

In 1998, this square, located on the north side of the new courthouse, was dedicated to Mary E. Smith-Hayward, an honorary member of Chadron Business and Professional Women's Club. (Photo courtesy of Breanne Thompson.)

This is a bird's-eye view of Chadron as well as Chadron State College in the mid-1930s. This photo was taken after Edna Work Hall opened in 1932 and before Crites Hall was built in 1938. (Photo courtesy of CSC.)

Chadron High School was built in 1968 and to this day remains the most modern school in the area. (Photo courtesy of Breanne Thompson.)

In 1888, Chadron's new high school building opened its doors to 227 eager pupils. (Postcard courtesy of Dawes County Historical Society.)

This is Chadron Middle School, 2004. (Photo courtesy of Breanne Thompson.)

In 1919, Jimmie Good established 100 lots north of the railroad tracks and named them Victory Heights. He donated one block from this area for the site of Kenwood School. (Photo courtesy of Breanne Thompson.)

This is an image of 2nd Street, taken in 2004. (Photo courtesy of Breanne Thompson.)

This is 2nd Street as it appeared after the blizzard of January 1949, when nearly 61 inches of snow fell. (Photo courtesy of Dawes County Historical Society.)

The First National Bank of Chadron, now located on the corner of 2nd and Main Streets, is Chadron's longest-running business operating under its original name. (Photo courtesy of Breanne Thompson.)

This is Main Street looking south to "C" hill. (Photo courtesy of Breanne Thompson.)

Built in 1928, the Chadron Community Hospital was said to be the first "community" hospital in all of Nebraska. It is located next to Wilson Park. (Photo courtesy of Breanne Thompson.)

E.P. Wilson was known for his help in organizing the Sioux Memorial Association. He spent many hours tending to the trees in the park that was named after him. (Photo courtesy of Breanne Thompson.)

Chadron Congregational Academy opened its doors in 1893 and closed them in 1910. In 1917, the building was torn down, but the bricks were salvaged, contributing to a barn for Chadron Normal School. (Photo courtesy of CSC, Slattery Collection.)

Driving First Stake for State Normal, at Chadron, Neb.
Pub. by M. M. Blanchard.

This postcard depicts the ground-breaking ceremony of the first building of Chadron State Normal College, which later became the administration building. (Postcard courtesy of Dawes County Historical Society.)

The original building for the Northwest Nebraska State Normal School later became known as the Administration Building for Chadron State College. (Photo courtesy of Chadron State College.)

This view of Chadron State College campus shows the hog house, chicken house, barn, gymnasium, administration building, and dormitory. (Photo courtesy of Chadron State College.)

Ivy Day celebrations were a highlight of Chadron State Normal students' lives. This is a picture of an Ivy Day celebration held on May 1, 1924. (Photo courtesy of Chadron State College.)

The Industrial Arts Shop was located in the basement on the east end of the Administration Building. (Photo courtesy of Chadron State College.)

A couple walks along the outlines of C-Hill. The C was placed on the hill behind the college in 1924, under the direction of T.A.F. Williams, a Math instructor at the college. The story goes that Williams had one of his former students who was working on his engineering degree help design the large letter. Williams and his wife walked along the lines of the C, much like this couple above, and also walked a distance to the north to see how it was going to look. As we can all still see, the idea was a success. For many years afterwards, it has been a tradition for members of the freshman class to repaint the C. Shortly after the cement was poured, the C motivated one student to write: "Men will come and men will pass. Class will follow class. But the C will remain in any event. Because it's made of Portland Cement." (Postcard courtesy of Dawes County Historical Society.)

This is a view of the Administration Building as it looked when Chadron State College was Nebraska State Normal College. (Postcard courtesy of Dawes County Historical Society.)

The lobbies of both the men's and women's dorms were social gathering spots during evenings. Pictured above is the lobby of Edna Work Hall. (Photo courtesy of CSC.)

The lobby of the men's hall at Chadron State Teachers College is now the lobby of Crites, which houses offices. (Photo courtesy of CSC.)

The old pool in Miller was removed during the remodeling of the building in the late 1990s. (Photo courtesy of CSC.)

This is a group of students in the days when Chadron State College was not a smoke-free campus. (Photo courtesy of CSC.)

The auditorium located in Memorial Hall has been a site for cultural events—from musical performances to theatrical productions—exposing students to the finer points of life. (Photo courtesy of CSC.)

The Mari Sandoz High Plains Heritage Center honors one of Nebraska's writers. (Photo courtesy of Deb Carpenter.)

This photo of the Chadron State College campus was taken in the fall of 1970, during the construction of what is now Burkhiser Technology Complex. (Photo courtesy of CSC.)

Burkhiser Technology Complex was named in honor of Donald Burkhiser, Professor of Industrial Arts from 1945 to 1978. Burkhiser Technology Complex was built in 1971, and it now hosts telecommunication classes. It also contains several shops and a lab room for the Industrial Technology Department. (Photo courtesy of Breanne Thompson.)

The High Rise Dormitory was completed in 1967. It is a 400-bed, 11-story residence hall that was originally intended for women. In 2001, High Rise was converted to a co-ed dorm. Kent Hall was named in honor of Albert E. Kent, who was the college Registrar from 1938 to 1963. Kent Hall opened in 1965. Andrews Hall Dormitory was named in honor of Lyle Andrews, a nationally-known science professor from Chadron State College. Andrews was built in 1966. (Photo courtesy of Breanne Thompson.)

Chadron State College students Shane Teichmeier, Dustin Harris, Lisa Weedin, Sully Serrano, and Breanne Thompson enjoy a visit to downtown Chadron. They mark the passage of time with the Blaine Hotel as their backdrop. (Photo courtesy of Breanne Thompson.)

Five

SURROUNDING AREAS

The beautiful panhandle of western Nebraska offers a vast array of tourist attractions that can spark the interest of any traveler. The area offers many sites of interest that range from past remains of bison to retired military forts. These attractions have kept the integrity of the past alive today.

A few of these attractions are still available to the touring public. They include Fort Robinson, which was used for many purposes—including a military post to monitor the actions of the Red Cloud Agency, a trading center, and later a German POW camp until 1958. It is also possible to see the site of Camp Sheridan, which was used to monitor the Spotted Tail Agency. Camp Sheridan is located in Beaver Valley between Chadron and Hay Springs.

The Museum of the Fur Trade is located a few miles east of Chadron. This museum boasts the largest collection of memorabilia from the fur-trading era in the world. In addition to the Museum of the Fur Trade, west of Chadron, near the geological anomaly Toadstool Park, is the Hudson-Meng bone bed, which contains literally thousands of bison bones.

These attractions are just a few of the extraordinary places that draw people from all over the world to Dawes County, Nebraska, each year. With scenic views of the hills and buttes, Chadron and the surrounding areas make a tranquil and beautiful place to visit. With friendly townspeople and interesting sites to see, the Chadron area makes a wonderful place to spend the summer. (Student co-authors: Tina Pearson, Sarah DeShaw, Lex Ravenscroft, Brice Bottorff, Mark Griffith, and Kent Kauffman.)

Beaver Wall

Chadron

▲ Sheri‹
Gat‹

Toadstool
Park

Whitney

Dawes ▪
County
Museum

Museum ▪
of the
Fur Trade

Hudson-Meng
Bonebed ▪

▲ Pants
▲ Butte

Lovers Leap ▲

●Crawford

Chadron
State
Park

Harrison

Fort
Robinson

▲ Crow Butte

Hay Spring

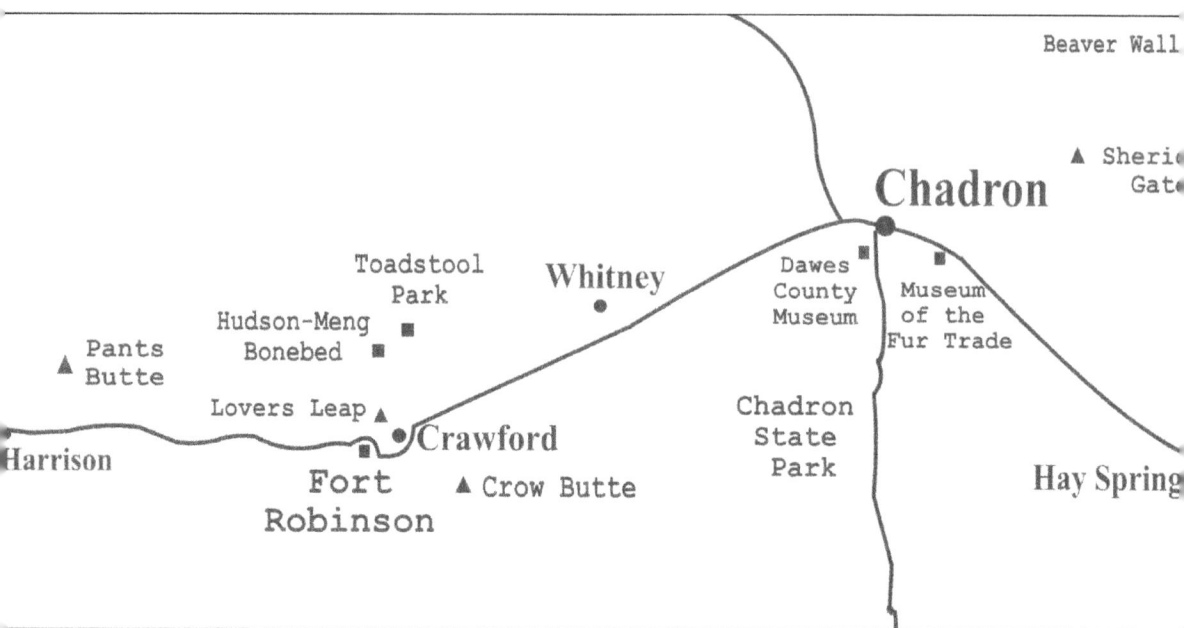

Tour the beautiful area surrounding Chadron. The following pages give closer glimpses of areas depicted here, beginning with the western edge, near Pants Butte, then working northeast to Beaver Valley. (Map courtesy of Lex Ravenscroft.)

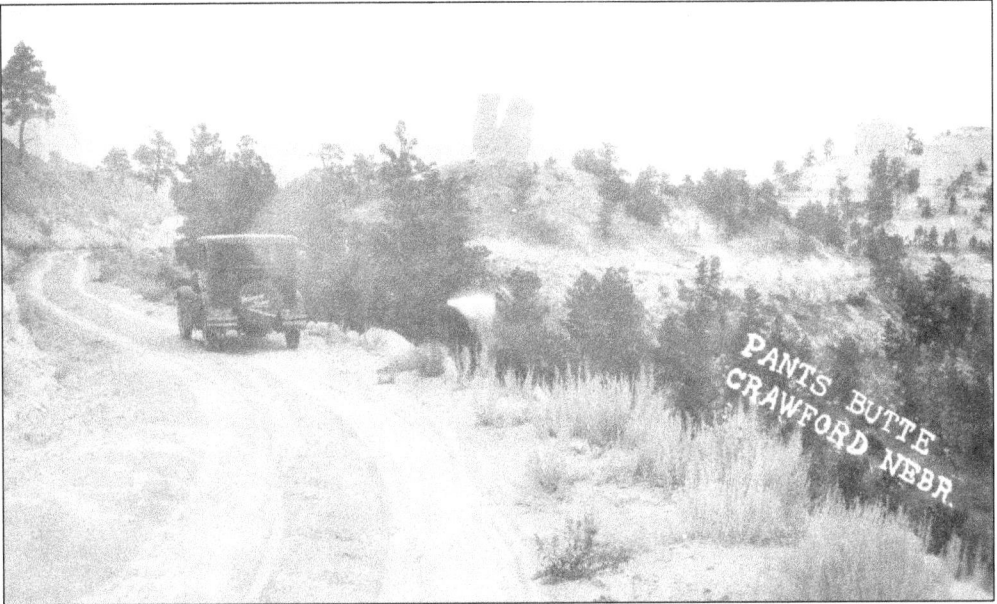

On the western edge of Dawes County lies the unique rock formation known as Pants Butte. (Postcard courtesy of Dawes County Historical Society.)

To the west of Crawford is the butte known as Saddle Rock. It stands as a reminder of one of the negative aspects of the area's history, known as a site of cross burning conducted by the Ku Klux Klan. (Postcard courtesy of Dawes County Historical Society.)

Fort Robinson officially became an establishment of the U.S. Government in March of 1874. The Lakota Sioux, Cheyenne, and Arapahoe Indians met here to discuss the approach of the white man and it became known as the Red Cloud Agency. The U.S Government thought it would be in their best interest to set up a camp here to prepare for the possible uprisings of the Indians. Eventually the Indians were forced to move to the Dakota Territory after the death of Crazy Horse. By March of 1943, the Red Cloud Agency had long been disbanded, and the fort was looking for a new reason to stay open. During World War II, a German POW camp and a military dog training facility were added. In 1955, the Game and Parks Commission acquired Fort Robinson's land in order to operate it as a museum and state park. (Photo courtesy of Deb Cottier.)

Fort Robinson's administration building was originally used for officers' housing and offices. Today, it can be rented for special events. (Postcard courtesy of Dawes County Historical Society.)

Pictured above are troops from Fort Robinson, participating in a parade held in Chadron. Some of them may have been Buffalo Soldiers. These soldiers were stationed at Fort Robinson for 18 years. The Buffalo Soldiers acquired their name from the Plains Indians. They were black troops who helped establish the new post during the 1887 fort expansion. These soldiers also made their mark in history by being some of the first cavalrymen sent to the Pine Ridge Reservation during the Ghost Dance troubles of 1890. (Photo courtesy of Dawes County Historical Society.)

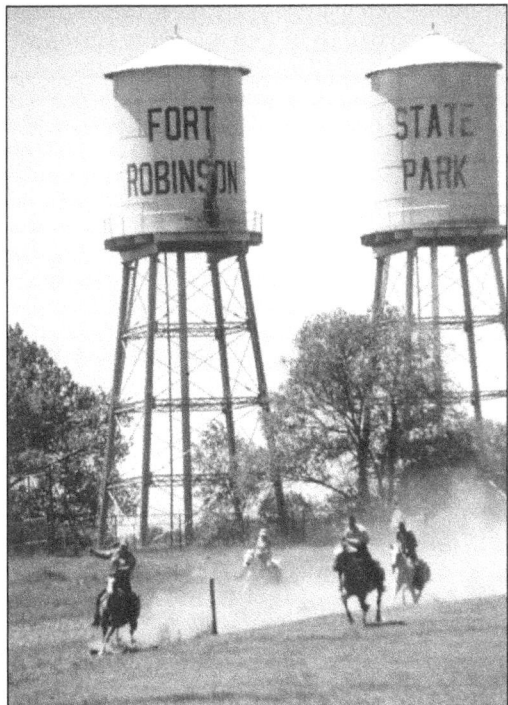

Horse races at Fort Robinson State Park are an activity that everyone seems to enjoy during the summer. Currently, Fort Robinson State Park has horses available for the general public to use on guided trail rides. (Photo courtesy of Deb Carpenter.)

Bird's Eye View of Crawford, Nebr.
Lovers Leap in Distance.

According to legend, a young brave wished to marry the chief's daughter, but the chief turned the young man away because he had not proven himself worthy. The young man then joined a war party to seek honor and the chief's approval. When word came back that the young man had been killed in battle, the young maiden fled to the hills, sang her death chant, and threw herself from the butte. The young man's body was brought into camp at the same time the young maiden's was brought back from the butte, and her father decided the couple should be joined in a marriage ceremony before being sent on their final journey to the spirit world. (Postcards courtesy of Dawes County Historical Society.)

LOVERS LEAP BUTTE, CRAWFORD, NEB.

114

Crow Butte, located west of Crawford, was named after a Crow Indian war party. The party, led by Chief White Bear, looted a trading post owned by James Bordeaux and ran off 82 horses and mules. During the small raid, a band of Brule Indians that were camped nearby at Beaver Creek heard of the incident and organized a rescue party. They pursued the Crow all day and then caught up with them at what is now known as Crow Butte. The war party took refuge on the butte and most of the Crow later escaped in the night. At least one Crow Indian was killed and very few horses were recovered. (Postcard courtesy of Dawes County Historical Museum.)

The rock formations that can currently be seen at Toadstool Park let us see why early explorers called the terrain "terres mauvais" or badlands. (Photo courtesy of Deb Carpenter.)

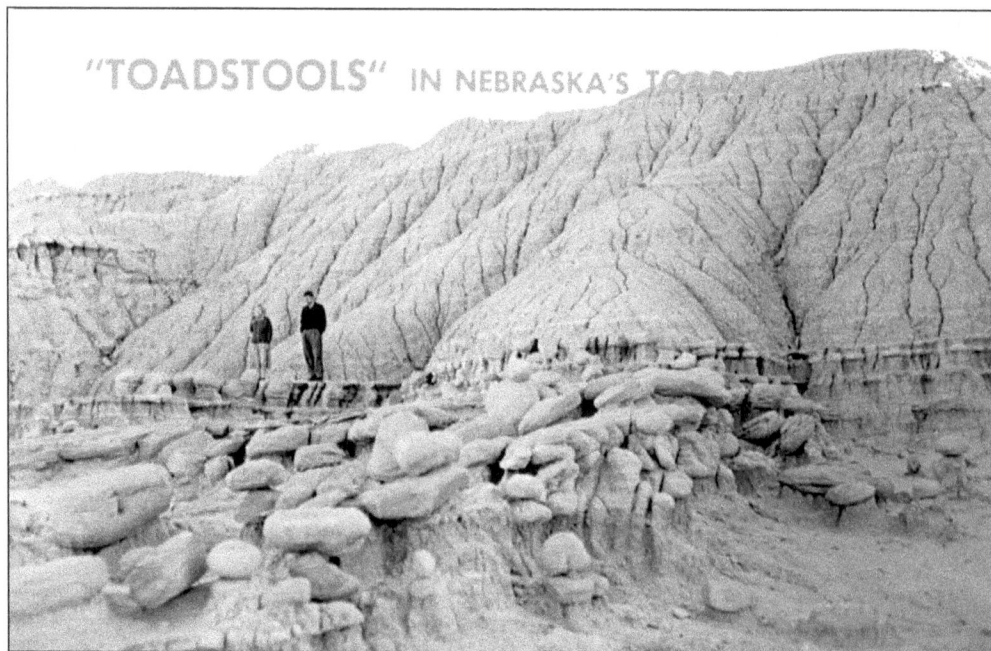

Erosion wears away at different layers in the sediment to give the land at Toadstool its unique formations. (Postcard courtesy of Dawes County Historical Society.)

The Hudson-Meng Bison Bonebed was discovered by two local ranchers, Bill Hudson and Albert Meng, in the early 1950s. The first excavation didn't start until 1971 when archaeologists discovered that the bone bed was approximately 8,000 to 10,000 years old and as many as 1,000 bison remains were found. Archaeologists and researchers still disagree to this day on exactly how the bison died. These pictures show volunteers excavating the bone bed in the 1970s. (Photos courtesy of Chadron State College.)

The Drifter Cookshack at the High Plains Homestead is on the road to the Hudson-Meng Bonebed. The High Plains Homestead offers respite for the traveler. (Photo courtesy of Drifter Cookshack.)

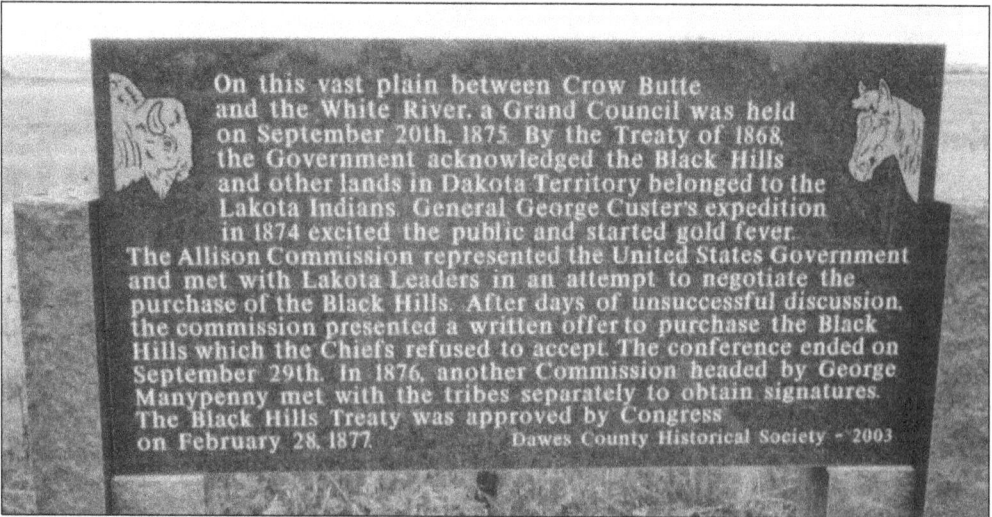

On this vast plain between Crow Butte and the White River, a Grand Council was held on September 20th, 1875. By the Treaty of 1868, the Government acknowledged the Black Hills and other lands in Dakota Territory belonged to the Lakota Indians. General George Custer's expedition in 1874 excited the public and started gold fever. The Allison Commission represented the United States Government and met with Lakota Leaders in an attempt to negotiate the purchase of the Black Hills. After days of unsuccessful discussion, the commission presented a written offer to purchase the Black Hills which the Chiefs refused to accept. The conference ended on September 29th. In 1876, another Commission headed by George Manypenny met with the tribes separately to obtain signatures. The Black Hills Treaty was approved by Congress on February 28, 1877.   Dawes County Historical Society - 2003

The monument for the 1875 Grand Council was dedicated September 20, 2003. The buffalo and horse are symbols of western history. (Photo courtesy of Rollin Curd.)

As Whitney boomed in 1887, the town grew in size and dozens of buildings, stores, and homes were built. This is a picture of the old Catholic church which later became Woodmen's Hall. (Photo courtesy of Dawes County Historical Society.)

Whitney is located on the south side of the White River. It was planned to be the county seat of Dawes County until Chadron boomed. This is one of the first churches built in Whitney. In the background is the schoolhouse. (Photo courtesy of Dawes County Historical Society.)

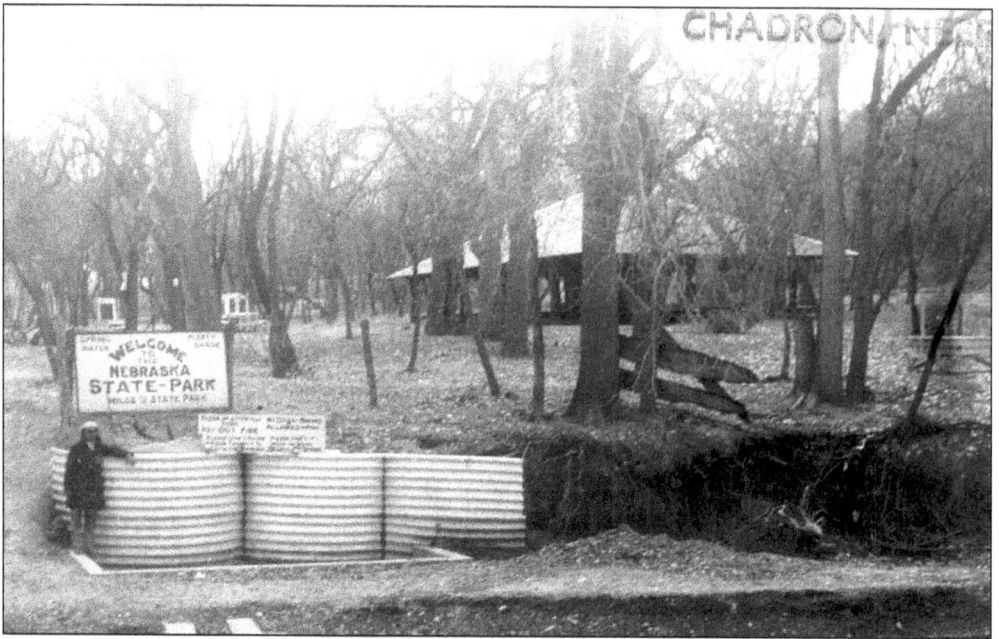

Chadron State Park was the first state park founded in Nebraska. It was founded in April of 1921 by Senator James Good and Representative George Snow, who both resided in Chadron. Currently, a valid vehicle entry permit is required to access the 974 acres. This picture was one of the first pictures of the entrance into the park. (Postcard courtesy of Dawes County Historical Society.)

The location of present-day Chadron State Park was once the site of a fierce battle between migratory Plains Indians and whites. After the battles ended, the land was disputed over by ranchers and homesteaders. This portrait portrays the highest point in Chadron State Park. It was taken eight miles south of Chadron. The altitude at the park is about 4,000 feet and the humidity is generally low. The nights are usually cool during the summer. (Postcard courtesy of Dawes County Historical Society.)

Pictured above and below is Good's Cabin. It is one of the first buildings built at Chadron State Park. Currently the park contains 22 cabins with kitchenettes, bathrooms, and showers. Today, the only part of the cabin that remains is a small part of its chimney. In addition to the cabins there are 70 electrical paved pads with 30 amp hook-ups for RV camping. The campgrounds include showers, a dump station, laundry facilities, picnic tables, grills, and playgrounds. For the more adventurous camper, tent camping areas are also available. (Postcard and photo courtesy of Dawes County Historical Society.)

Visitors to Chadron State Park are seen here enjoying the recreational activity of swimming in the cool lake. The lake is no longer used for swimming, but is currently stocked with trout. Today, Chadron State Park is a tourist attraction where people come to go trout fishing, camping, mountain biking, bird watching, horseback riding, and take part in a variety of other outdoor activities. (Postcard courtesy of Dawes County Historical Society.)

Dawes County Museum is located three miles south of Chadron. The museum houses a variety of memorabilia from the early period in the history of Dawes County. The grounds contain a log house and barn, an 1890s school house, and a pioneer church. The museum itself is 9,000 square feet. Chadron State College students pose for a picture after visiting the museum. (Photo courtesy of Deb Carpenter.)

The Museum of the Fur Trade, located a few miles east of Chadron, was once the location of a French fur trading post. Today it is the most extensive museum on the fur trade in the world. It is funded by private donations and has recently been renovated by volunteer labor. The building seen here is the renovated trading post, a short walking distance from the museum. (Photo courtesy of Brice Bottorff.)

Sheridan Gates are two large buttes named for General Philip H. Sheridan. They mark the boundary between Dawes County and Sheridan County. This photo was shot from the east side, looking west into Dawes County. (Photo courtesy of Deb Carpenter.)

Many of the historic sites that are no longer in existence were once situated along the Beaver Wall, located between Chadron and Pine Ridge. (Photo courtesy of Deb Carpenter.)

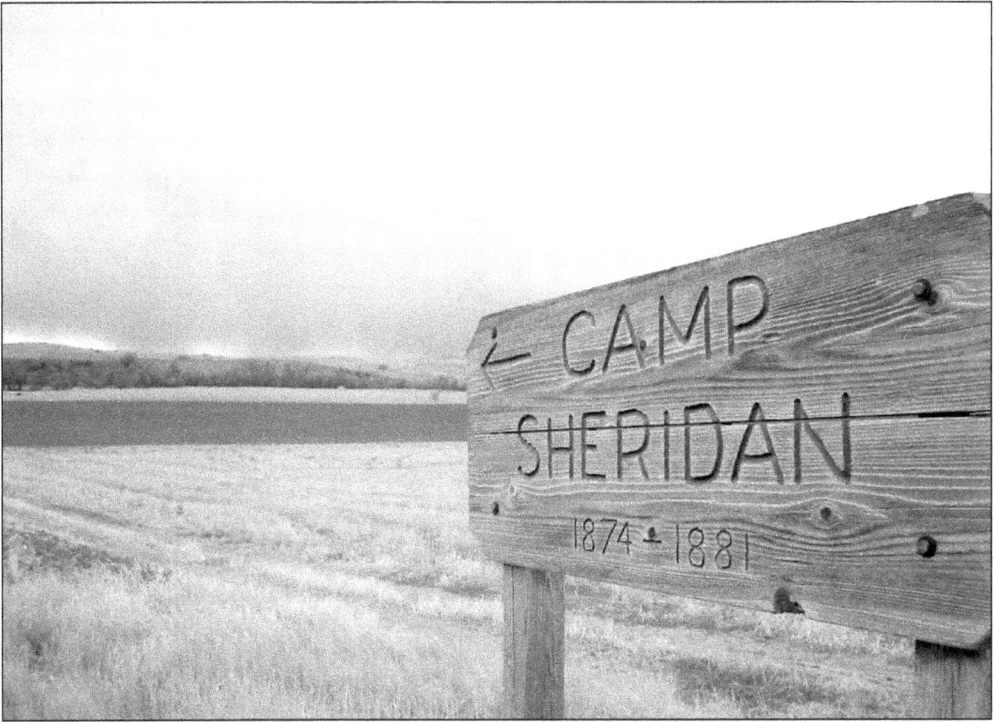

Camp Sheridan, once located in Beaver Valley, was a military post that monitored the Spotted Tail Agency. It was built at the same time Camp Robinson was built in 1874. Because of problems with flooding and poor foundations, Camp Sheridan was re-built more than once. The camp consisted of three barracks and several officers' quarters. It was very self-sufficient in the fact that it had a bakery, trading post, blacksmith shop, sawmill, and carpentry shop as well. The camp was torn down in 1881 and all quartermasters, commissary, and other supplies were shipped to Fort Robinson. Printed here is an illustration that shows what the camp used to look like. (Photo courtesy of Deb Carpenter. Map courtesy of Sarah DeShaw.)

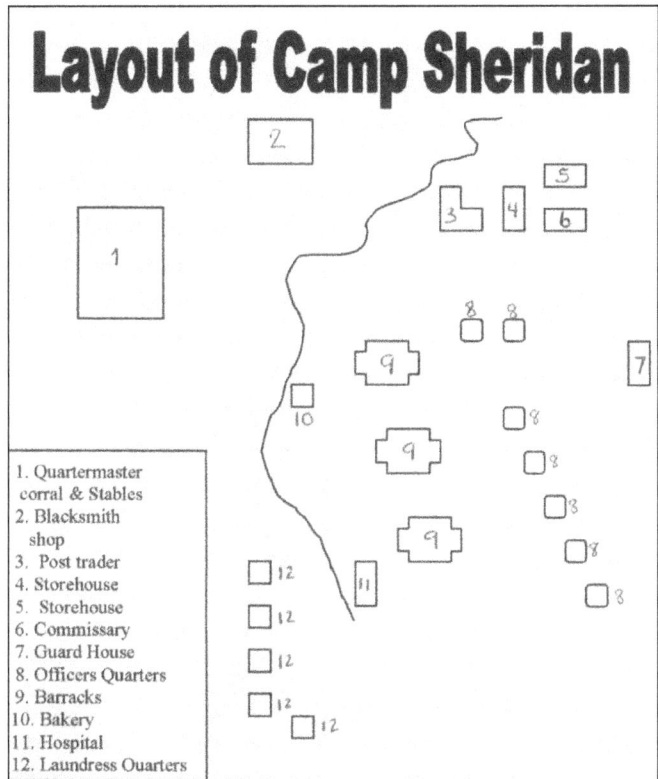

Layout of Camp Sheridan

1. Quartermaster corral & Stables
2. Blacksmith shop
3. Post trader
4. Storehouse
5. Storehouse
6. Commissary
7. Guard House
8. Officers Quarters
9. Barracks
10. Bakery
11. Hospital
12. Laundress Quarters

To the average person just passing by, this crevasse wouldn't seem unusual, but it is in fact an old warrior shelter. Indians would use hiding spaces like this to elude their enemies or to seek shelter during storms. (Photo courtesy of Mabell Kadlecek.)

Many Native American tribes placed the bodies of their departed loved ones in trees or on scaffolds. This burial tree held several bodies, which weighed the branches down. The tree was sickened by Dutch Elm disease that ran through the area during the 1980s, died, rotted, and is no longer standing. The body of Crazy Horse was placed in another tree near this one. Crazy Horse was killed at Fort Robinson and his body brought to Beaver Valley. His body was removed by his parents and taken to a secret location for burial. (Photo courtesy of Mabell Kadlecek.)

BIBLIOGRAPHY

Buecker, Thomas. "History of Camp Sheridan, Nebraska." *Journal of America's Military Post.* 1995.

Chadron Narrative History Project Committee. *Chadron, Nebraska Centennial History: 1885–1985.* Freeman, SD: Pine Hill Press, 1985.

Clark, LaVerne Harrell. *Re-Visiting the Plains Indian Country of Mari Sandoz.* Marvin, SD: The Blue Cloud Quarterly, 1977.

Curd, Rollin C. *A History of the Boundaries of Nebraska and Indian-Surveyor Stories.* Chadron, NE: Boundaries Publishing Company, 1999.

Graff, Jane, Project Director. *Nebraska: Our Towns. The Panhandle.* Dallas, TX: Taylor Publishing Co., 1988.

Grange Jr., Roger T. "Fort Robinson: Outpost on the Plains." Reprint from *Nebraska History,* Volume 39, No. 3, September, 1958.

Griffith, George V. *The Chadron Public Library: A Centennial History, 1889–1989.*

Hanson Jr., Charles, and Veronica Sue Walters. "The Early Fur Trade in Northwestern Nebraska." *Nebraska History,* 57 (Fall 1976). Reprint in booklet form, 1985.

Herman, Jake. *Pictorial Book of the Oglala Sioux.* 1968.

Kadlecek, Edward and Mabell. *To Kill an Eagle.* Boulder, CO: Johnson Publishing Company, 2000.

Kadlecek, Mabell. *Beaver Valley 1962–1994.* Unpublished, 2004.

Mills, Rick W. and James J. Reisdorff. *The High, Dry and Dusty.* David City, NE: South Platte Press, 1992.

"National Scenic Byways, Nebraska Gold Rush Byways, Sidney-Deadwood Trail." http://www.byways.org.

Paul, R. Eli, editor. *The Nebraska Indian Wars Reader 1865–1877*. Lincoln, NE: University of Nebraska Press, 1998.

Radcliffe, Rip. *The Chadron to Chicago Cowboy Horse Race of 1893*. Chadron, NE: B&B Printing, 1984.

Rhoads, Minnie Alice. *A Stream Called Deadhorse*. Chadron, NE: Chadron Printing Co., 1957.

Shepherd, Dr. Allen, et al., editors. *Man of Many Frontiers: The Diaries of "Billy the Bear" Iaeger*. Omaha, NE: Making History, 1994.

Shumway, Grant L. *History of Western Nebraska and Its People*. Volume 2: Lincoln, NE: The Western Publishing and Engraving Company, 1921.

"The Cowboys Are Off." *Dawes County Journal* 16 June 1893: 1.

United States Department of Agriculture. *Hudson-Meng Bison Bonebed*. Brochure. April 2000.

United States Department of Agriculture. *Toadstool Geologic Park*. Brochure.

"Walking Tour of Historic Chadron." http://www.chadron.com/history/

Watson, George D. *Prairie Justice. 1885–1985: A One-Hundred Year Study of the Legal System of Chadron and Dawes County*. Chadron, NE: B & B Printing, 1985.

Visit us at
arcadiapublishing.com

....

www.ingramcontent.com/pod-product-compliance
Lightning Source LLC
Chambersburg PA
CBHW080608110426
42813CB00006B/1445